EXPERIMENTS
with
WATER

Contents

1. Water Around Us 5
2. Let Us Study Water 8
3. The Three States of Water 12
4. Floating and Sinking 18
5. Surface Tension 22
6. Earth's Gift for Living Beings 28

Water Around Us

All living beings need water to survive. Water is used for drinking, watering plants and cleaning.

Water covers more than 70% of the earth's surface. Water can be seen in ponds, lakes, streams, rivers, seas and oceans. A lot of it is unseen too.

A large part of the unseen water is hidden as underground water. It can be reached by digging a well or a hole in the ground. During rains, rainwater seeps into the soil. Clayey soil has lots of pores in it to hold this water. Rocks can hold very little rainwater.

Make your own cloud

You will need:

- a glass jar, with a mouth wide enough for your fist to pass through
- a sheet of rubber made from slitting a large balloon
- some chalk dust
- a rubber band

1. Pour about an inch of water into the jar.
2. Place the rubber sheet over the mouth of the jar. Keep it in place with a book. Leave it covered for ten minutes.
3. Put the chalk dust into the jar and quickly secure the rubber sheet tightly over the mouth of the jar with the rubber band.

4. Push your fist against the rubber sheet until it is inside the jar. This will warm the air inside the jar and make it hold more water vapour.
5. After ten seconds, remove your fist from the rubber sheet. This will suddenly cool the air in the jar. Cold air holds less water vapour than warm air. The extra water will condense around the particles of chalk dust. As a result, a cloud will form inside the jar.

The tiny water droplets in a cloud come together and join to form larger water drops. When they become too heavy, they fall out of the clouds as rain.

If it is very cold inside a cloud, the drops of water inside the cloud freeze to form crystals of ice which stick together. When the air below the cloud is also cold, the ice crystals fall as snow.

Try this

To check this, fill two plant pots, one with clay and the other with sand. Pour a glass of water into each pot and see how long it takes the water to seep out of the pots through the holes below.

The rest of the unseen water is in the atmosphere and in the clouds, in the form of vapour. Due to the sun's heat, water from rivers and seas becomes water vapour. As the water vapour rises up, it cools and becomes tiny drops of water. These droplets collect around dust particles in the air to form clouds.

Make yourself some frost

You will need:

- a tall can
- some ice
- salt

1. Pack the tin can with alternate layers of ice and salt. The ice should be twice the amount of salt.
2. When it is full, notice what happens to the can on the outside.

High reaches of mountains receive regular snowfall in winter. In summer, the snow melts to form streams. Streams run down mountain slopes and join to form rivers. Rivers fall into seas and oceans. During the monsoons, rainwater flows into the ground and into lakes, rivers and seas.

Thus we find that water goes through a long journey from the earth to the sky and back. This is called the water cycle.

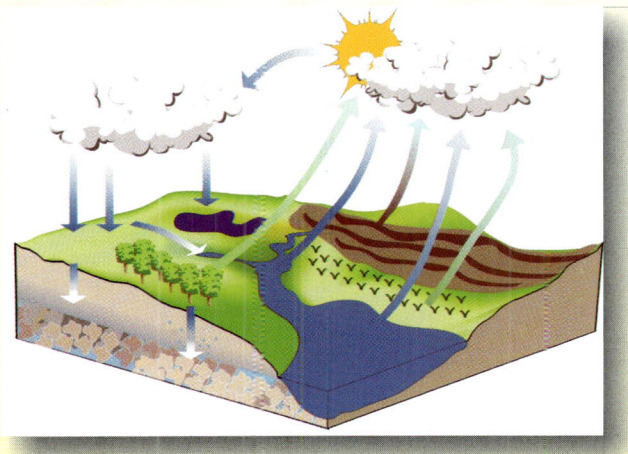

Let Us Study Water

There is so much water around us that we hardly ever bother to give it a thought. It is time that we do so.

What is water like?

- Water is a liquid.
- It has no shape. It takes the shape of the container in which it is kept.
- Water has no colour, no taste, no odour. Water is transparent.

What is water made of?

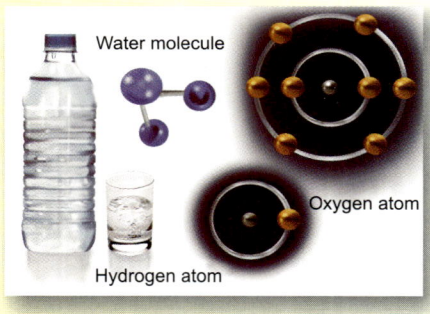

- Water is made up of two gases. One is oxygen, the gas we breathe in. The other is hydrogen, a very light invisible gas.
- Each water molecule is made up of two atoms of hydrogen and one atom of oxygen. Scientists call water H_2O.

Water flows downwards

Have you ever watched the streams made by rainwater? You will notice that all these streams invariably flow into the gutter or to the lowest point in the locality. Water always flows down a slope. This is due to the force of gravity.

Water cannot flow on a flat surface and thus stays there.

Water finds its own level

1. Cut a plastic bottle at both ends to get a cylindrical shape. Hold it in a container of water.
2. Keep pouring water into it. Watch the water level inside as well as outside the cylinder. You will find that however much you try, the water inside the cylinder can never be at a level higher than that in the container.

Water applies pressure

When water is pushed, it flows more quickly. Water pressure gets greater, the deeper you go in it.

Test this out in a swimming pool

As you go deeper while swimming, your ears may hurt. This is because the water presses in on your eardrums with a greater pressure.

Another test for pressure

1. Take a plastic bottle and make three holes in it at different levels.
2. Cover the holes with a strip of plaster.
3. Now fill the bottle with water.
4. Strip the plaster off quickly. The water will spurt from the holes. The hole which is at the lowest level has the biggest jet of water. This is because water pressure is greatest at the deepest level.

Water cannot be compressed

If you apply pressure on water, water does not shrink in volume. Instead, it carries and distributes the pressure. This idea is used in hydraulic presses and elevators.

Make a simple hydraulic press

You will need:

- a glass container
- paraffin wax
- water
- 2 glass tubes, one bent and the other straight
- a square piece of cardboard

1. Fill half the container with water.
2. Pour molten paraffin wax into the water. It will stay on the water surface.
3. Hold the bent tube in the water and the straight tube in the wax, as the wax cools.
4. When the wax solidifies, it forms an air-tight piston. Fix the cardboard to the top of the piston and place a weight on it.
5. Blow gently through the bent tube.

   The piston with the weight will start rising!

Try this

Can water dilute all liquids? Try mixing water in oil.

Make a Chinese wash painting

1. Draw the outline of a picture you want to paint.
2. Wet the drawing paper.
3. Put a little thick coat of colour on the paper.
4. Wet your brush and spread the colour. Watch the subtle shades as the colour spreads.
5. Apply other colours, dilute them by adding water and complete your painting.

Water dilutes

Water can dilute other liquids. That is, water can make other liquids less strong or less concentrated.
1. Take a glass of concentrated sugar solution. Taste it.
2. Mix it with an equal amount of water. Taste it again. Is the sweetness less?

   This is because water has reduced the concentration of sugar in the solution.

Water dissolves

Water is a solvent. Many things dissolve in it. Check this.

You will need:
- 6 glasses of water
- sand, salt, sugar, grass, earth, red colour powder
- a spoon

Add one spoonful of each ingredient in the six respective glasses of water.
Stir and see which ones dissolve.
Note the change in the colour of the water.
Things like salt, sugar and coloured powder dissolve in water. Sand and grass do not.
Look at the glass in which earth was dissolved. Is there anything at the bottom of the glass that has not dissolved?

 Try this

Keep on adding sugar to a glass of water.
Will all the sugar dissolve? What happens if you heat the sugar-water syrup? Does more sugar dissolve now?

The Three States of Water

We think of water as a liquid. However, water can be a solid or a gas. Solid water is called ice. Water freezes into ice at 0°C. Water in the gaseous state is called steam. Water turns into steam at 100°C. Let us take a closer look at the three states of water.

You will need:
- a kettle
- some ice cubes
- a serving spoon

1. Put the ice cubes in the kettle. Place the kettle over low heat. Keep the lid open so that you can see the reaction inside the kettle.
   Presently, the ice will melt into water. It changes from the solid to the liquid state.
2. When all the ice has melted, put the lid on the kettle, and increase the heat. Can you see steam coming out of the spout? Water has changed from the liquid to the gaseous state.
3. Wrap a towel around the handle of the spoon, and hold it in front of the spout. Can you see the drops of water? The steam is becoming water again!
   If you can collect these water drops and put them in the freezer, it will change to ice again.

It is not necessary to boil water to change it to the gaseous state. The heat of the earth causes water to become water vapour and disappear into the air. This happens all the time. The sun heats the rivers and seas.

Heat causes water to evaporate. Check this.

You will need:
- 2 saucers of the same size
- a tablespoon
- water

1. Place one saucer under direct sunlight and the other in a cool place.
2. Put one tablespoon of water in each saucer. The water in the sunlight will evaporate faster than the water in the cool place.

Water evaporates faster from a larger surface

1. Place a spoonful of water under direct sunlight. Prop up the handle so that the water does not spill out.
2. Pour a spoonful of water into a saucer and place the saucer under sunlight.

The water in the saucer will evaporate faster than the water in the spoon, even though the amount is the same.

If a bowl of hot soup is too hot to eat, pour the soup into a shallow plate. What happens?

You have just learnt that water evaporates faster from a larger surface. Is it then true that faster evaporation helps in faster cooling? In other words, does it mean that evaporation causes cooling?

It surely does. Otherwise why would you feel cold when after playing, you stand under/near the fan to evaporate your sweat?

Fanning also helps evaporation by circulating fresh air over the surface from where evaporation takes place.

A substance dissolved in water is left behind when the water evaporates. That is why rainwater formed by water from muddy streams is pure and clear.

Make some salt crystals

You will need:

- a glass jar
- a spoon
- hot water
- salt
- thread
- a short stick or an old pencil
- plasticine
- a piece of black paper
- a magnifying glass
- a sheet of white paper

1. Place the spoon in the jar. Then pour some hot water into the jar. Remove the spoon.
2. Add salt, a little at a time, and watch it dissolve. Continue adding salt till no more can be dissolved in the water. You will know this when you see some salt remaining at the bottom of the jar.
3. Tie a length of thread to the pencil. At the other end, stick a small ball of plasticine.
4. Hang the thread in the salt solution for a few days. Salt crystals will form as the water evaporates.

Place some crystals on the black paper and study them through the magnifying glass. What shape are the crystals?

You must have noticed that clothes take longer to dry on a hot humid day than on a dry day. Do you know why?

Evaporation is slow if the amount of water vapour in the atmosphere is more. The amount of water vapour in the air is called *humidity*. You can measure humidity with a hygrometer.

Make your own hygrometer

You will need:
- a wooden stand
- a cotton reel
- a straw
- a strand of long hair
- a board pin
- a card
- sellotape

1. Fix the reel to the wooden board as shown in the picture.
2. Tape the hair to the top of the stand. Run the hair over the reel.
3. Stick the card to the stand under the reel. Pin one end of the straw on the card and tie the hair near the other end.

The hair will be longer when the air is wet than when the air is dry. As humidity changes, the hair will stretch or shrink, moving the straw either up or down.

Warm air can contain more water vapour than cool air. Air can be cooled to a point at which it can no longer hold all the water vapour it contains. When this happens, water vapour forms water droplets. This is *condensation*.

At night, leaves, grass and stones become cold. The air next to these objects also gets cold at night. The cool air cannot hold its water vapour and so dew drops are formed.

Make dew drops at home

You will need:
- a shiny tin can
- ice cubes
- water

1. Fill the can with water. Wipe the outside of the can dry.
2. Add ice cubes and watch the outer surface of the can. Can you see dews forming? If necessary, add more ice to the water.

Water expands when it freezes

1. Fill a glass with water to half the level.
2. Place it in the freezer. Once frozen, you will notice that the ice sticks up above the previous water level. This is because water expands as it freezes.
3. If you melt the ice, the water will fall back to its original level.

Water pipes burst during extreme winters. Do you know why?

Remember

Never keep a filled glass bottle in the freezer. It might crack when the liquid inside freezes.

Try this

On a very cold day, breathe out from your mouth. You can see your breath. Why?

Ice is lighter than water

It might surprise you, but ice is lighter than water. When water freezes into solid ice, it becomes lighter than when it was liquid.

This is important to plants and fish living in water. When ponds and rivers freeze, the ice floats. So living things in the water are not affected.

If ice were heavier than water, then freezing would take place from the bottom upwards.

Try this

1. Pour a cup of water in a measuring jug, and put it in the freezer. Note the level of water. When freezing, note that the freezing takes place from the top.
2. Once frozen, take it out. Break the extra ice that is above the level you had noted.
3. Keep the jug outside. Let the ice melt. Where is the water level now?
4. Pour the water back into the cup. Is it not less than a cup? So, one cup of ice is equal to less than one cup of water, which means, ice is lighter than water.

Floating and Sinking

Take a bucket and fill it with water. Drop into it a collection of small items (a stone, a plastic toy, a nail, some foil, an empty matchbox, candle, etc.). Note the things that sink and those that float.

Water makes things float by pushing them in the upward direction. This is its buoyancy or upthrust.

If you try to push a toy or a tin with its lid on, into a bucket of water, and let go of it quickly, you will notice that it comes to the surface of the water. Can you feel the upthrust on the can?

An interesting fact

If you drop an iron nail into a bucket of water, it sinks. But surprisingly, a ship which is also made of iron, floats on the water. What is the secret?

Let us try to find out

You will need:
- a sheet of silver foil
- a container of water

1. Make a boat out of the silver foil.
2. Place it in a bucket of water. It floats.
3. Crush the foil into a small, tight ball and drop it into the bucket. It sinks.

The shape of the boat helps it stay afloat.

Now take a balloon or a polythene bag. Fill it with water and tie the end. Put it in a bucket of water. What do you notice?

The balloon neither sinks nor floats. Do you know why?

The golden rule of floating

A body floats in water when the upthrust on the body is equal to the weight of the body.
Is it that there is no upthrust on things that do not float? No, it only means that a body will sink when the upthrust on it is less than its weight.

Who found this out?

Archimedes, an ancient Greek scientist did. While studying upthrusts, he found that the upthrust was always equal to the weight of the water it pushes aside or displaces. This is called the Archimedes' Principle. Did you know that this idea struck him while taking a bath in a bathtub?

Remember

The Archimedes' Principle is true not only for water, but for all liquids and gases which are at rest.

Measure the volume of your body

1. Fill your bathtub three-quarters with water.
2. Mark the water-level on the tub with a crayon.
3. Step into the tub, and once seated, mark the new water level. You will notice that the water has been pushed up. The space between the two marks is the volume of your body.

Measure the volume of a stone

1. Take a measuring jug.
2. Put 400 ml of water into it.
3. Carefully put a pebble into the jug and note the new water-level. The difference between the old and new level is the volume of the stone.

If the level in the measuring jug has risen by 100 ml, then what is the volume of the pebble?

*One millilitre is the same amount as one cubic centimetre.

Submarines are special, covered boats that can go under water. When a submarine is at the surface, its tanks are full of air which keep it afloat. To make it sink, water is pumped into the tanks. The tanks are filled until the submarine neither floats nor sinks, but remains at the required depth. They have to be very strong so that they are not crushed by the great pressure underwater.

Make your own submarine

Take a plastic bottle and fill it up with water, leaving a little space at the top. Take the plastic cap of a ballpoint pen and stick a ball of plasticine at the end. Carefully put the cap into the bottle and screw on the lid tightly. The cap will float near the surface of the water.

You can make the cap float or sink by simply squeezing the sides of the bottle.

Can you guess why this happens?

Float an egg?

1. Place an egg carefully in a glass of fresh water. You will see that it stays at the bottom of the glass.
2. Now add salt to the glass of water. Look at this picture to see what happens.

An interesting fact

Ships ride higher in ocean water which is salty, than they do in the fresh water of rivers.

Oil floats on water

It is possible to float one liquid on another. Oil floats on water. This is why it is difficult to put out a petrol fire with water. The petrol floats on top of the water and keeps burning.

That is why oil spills in the sea or ocean or oil slicks from oil tankers are so dangerous. The spilt oil can cause massive damage to marine life. It can also float ashore and pollute beaches.

Do you remember the extent of damage caused by the oil slicks during the Gulf War in 1990?

Surface Tension

A tomato has a skin to it. So does a grape. The surface of water has a skin to it too.
Sounds unbelievable, doesn't it?

Check this

1. Fill a glass to its brim with water.
2. Drop a needle into it. You would imagine that some water would have spilt out, but it did not. In fact, you can add quite a few needles to the glass of water.
3. Now examine the water closely. Instead of it flowing out of the glass, it seems to be held in by a stretched invisible skin under tension or strain. This is called *surface tension*.

It is important to understand that water does not really have a skin like hot milk. It is only the top layer of water molecules behaving like skin.

Now lower a needle (placed on a fork) carefully into a glass of water. The needle will actually float when you take the fork away.

Lift the surface of the water

1. Use a piece of fine wire to make a hook. File the point of the hook until it is very sharp.
2. Fill a glass with water.
3. Place your eye on level with the surface of the water. Put the hook under water and gently raise the point to the surface. When carefully done, the point will lift the surface skin of the water slightly.

Some water insects walk upside-down, suspended from the water's surface. Their legs also lift the skin of the surface slightly.

Bubbling fun

Soap, when thoroughly mixed with water, makes the surface of the water more elastic. This is how you can make bubbles out of soapy water.

1. Mix 3 tablespoons of soap powder with 4 cups of warm water. Let it stand for a while.
2. Make a bubble pipe by making four slits at the end of a straw. Fold out the four flaps.
3. Dip the straw into the surface of the liquid and blow gently. You will get beautiful bubbles.

Did you note the shape of the bubbles? Soap bubbles are invariably circular because this shape gives least surface tension.

Soap rings

You will need:
- a wire
- a red thread
- soap solution
- a bucket of water

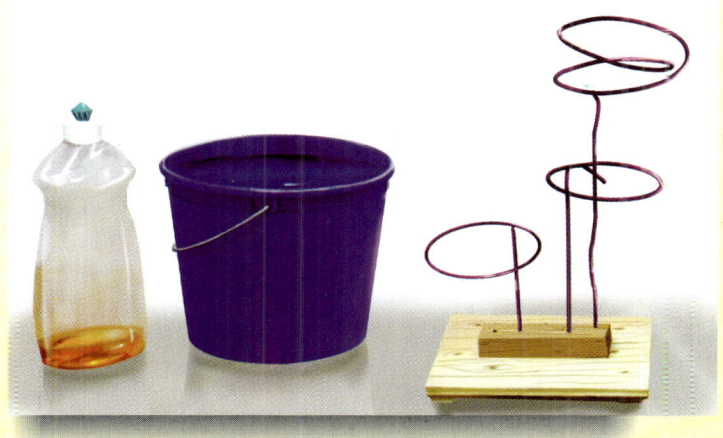

1. Bend the end of the wire into a ring.
2. Tie the red thread loosely across the ring.
3. Dip the ring in soap water. You will get a soap film.
4. Break the soap film on one side of the thread. What do you find?
5. Tie a loop in the thread. Dip it in soap water and break the film inside the loop. What happens?

In both cases, the soap films that remained in the ring are under strain and try to become as small as possible. So they pull the thread towards them.

We know that water takes the shape of the vessel in which it is kept. If poured on a surface, water spreads. Is this always true?

Does water have any shape?

You will need:
- two clean plastic plates
- some oil
- water

1. Pour a little water on one plate. The water spreads and wets the plate. The surface tension of water being low, the plate pulls the water towards it. So the water cannot take any particular shape.
2. Smear the other plate with oil. Now pour a little water on it. What do you notice? The surface tension between oil and water is high. So the plate can no longer pull the water and make it spread. Instead, the water breaks into small circular drops.

Have you seen water drops on a lotus leaf?

Soap affects surface tension

Detergents drastically reduce the surface tension between oil and water. So you use detergents to remove grease from utensils.

1. Rinse a plate absolutely clean. Fill the plate with cold water and wait till it is absolutely still.
2. Sprinkle some talcum powder over the surface of the water.
3. Touch a piece of wet soap to the water near the edge of the plate. You notice that the powder is attracted to the opposite side of the plate. As soap reduces the surface tension of the water which it touches, the powder is drawn to the side where the surface tension is more.

Moving matches

1. Arrange some matches like spokes, on a bowl of water, as shown.
2. Dip a piece of soap in the centre. The matches will move outwards.
3. Now dip a piece of blotting paper in the centre. Watch the matches as they close in.

Did you know ?

Trees and plants have very thin tubes running through them? They draw water upwards by capillarity.

Do all things absorb water?

You will need:
- sponge
- blotting paper
- newspaper
- a paper napkin

1. Place these items on a table.
2. Pour a few drops of water on each of them. What do you notice?

The sponge, blotting paper, newspaper and paper napkin will all absorb or take in the water. Can you guess why this happened? There are tiny pores in these objects that suck in water due to surface tension. This is known as the *capillary effect*. It can be seen if you dip a piece of chalk in ink or a towel in water. What about the cloth pieces from a raincoat or an umbrella?

A bi-coloured flower

Take a white flower and carefully divide its stem into two parts. Fill a glass with water and another with ink. Dip half the stem in the glass of water and the other half in the ink. If you look at the flower after a few hours, you will be in for a surprise.

Check this

1. Take two glasses. Fill one with water and place it at a higher level than the other glass, as shown.
2. Twist a wet handkerchief and put it over the glasses, so that it touches the bottom of the higher glass, but only the top of the other glass. Leave them for a few hours.
   Where do you think the water is?

Paper tie-and-dye

You will need:
- some white paper napkins
- red, green and blue ink

1. Fold the napkins.
2. Dip one end of one of the napkins in red ink.
3. Dip the other end in green ink and the middle portion in blue ink.
4. Dry and unfold to find a beautiful pattern. Be imaginative and make new designs.

Waterproof materials

Some materials are waterproof. They keep water out.

Take squares of kitchen foil, greaseproof paper, waterproof fabric and plastic. Test to see if they are all water-resistant.

Materials which absorb water, can also be made waterproof, by coating them with oil, wax or plastic.

1. Take a piece of paper and brush it with fevicol. Let it dry.
2. Put a drop of water on the fevicol. What do you observe?

Find out

Can you guess why water flows off a duck's back?
Ducks have oily feathers. So water does not soak into their feathers.

Earth's Gift for Living Beings

Water is earth's gift for living beings It is one of the most useful things. Think of ways how water is useful to you.

How many uses of water can you think of?

Did you take into account the use of water in industries? Even though there are 500 million cubic metres of water on earth, it is not equally distributed in all areas. Neither is rainfall uniform throughout all the regions of the earth. Some parts of the earth, like the tropical rain forests get rain for about eight months of the year, while the arid desert areas hardly get any rainfall.

Water provides power. Fix a hosepipe to a tap. Cover the end of the hosepipe with your thumb, and then open the tap. Can you feel the pressure of the water? If you remove your thumb, the water will gush out. This water force is used to generate electricity.

Did you know?

There is no water on the moon.

Reservoirs store water. Dams are built across rivers to make artificial lakes or reservoirs. In places where rainfall is not sufficient, stored water from reservoirs is used for irrigation.

In hydroelectric power stations, water is made to fall from a height and push against the blades of a turbine. A turbine is very much like a water wheel. The wheel turns make the generator work, and as a result, electricity is produced.

Make your own water wheel

1. Cut a circle out of card paper and draw five sections on it.
2. Tape it to the end of an old cotton reel.
3. Cut out five vanes.
4. Fold the tabs of the vanes. Stick the vanes after placing them carefully in position on the lines of the circle and on the reel.
5. Push a straw through the centre of the reel, so that it spins freely.
6. Spin the wheel under running water.

vane

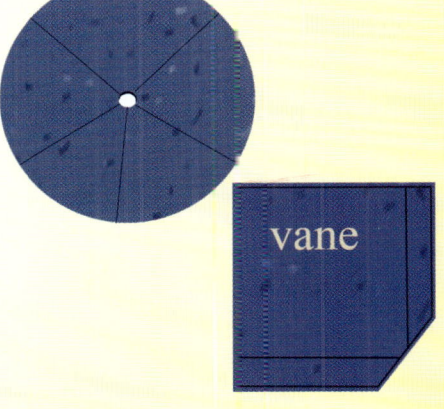

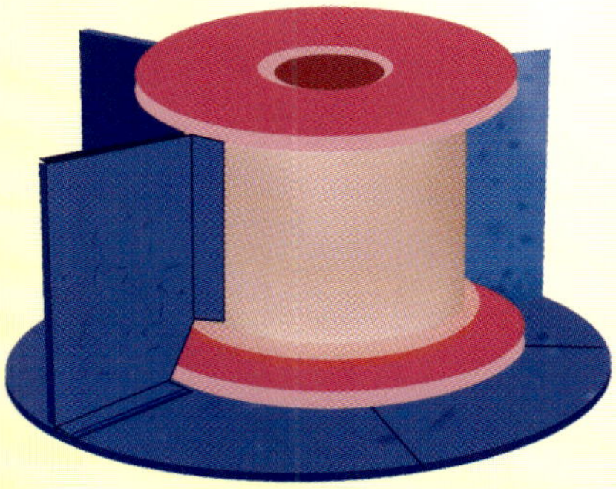

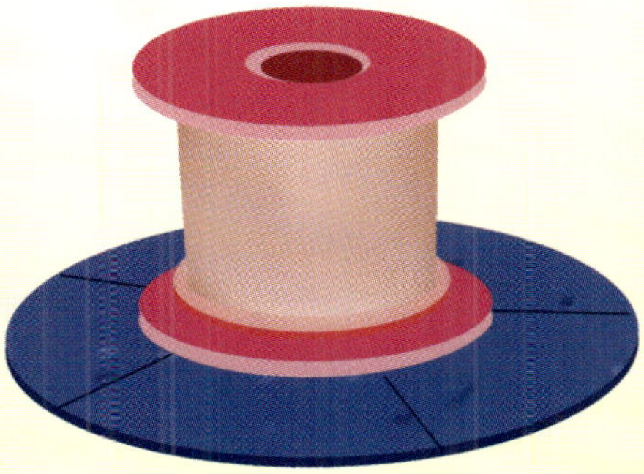

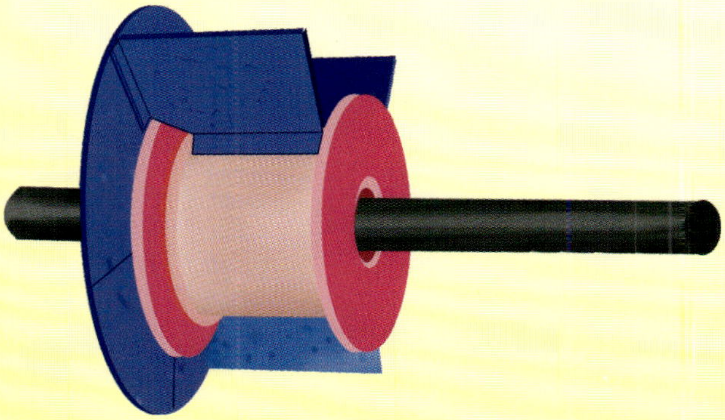

Take care of earth's gift – otherwise it may not last forever.

Conserve water

Remember to close taps tightly. Open a tap so that it just drips. Hold a glass under it and note the time required to fill the glass with water. From this, can you calculate the amount of water wasted per day if there are 100 leaking taps in your locality?

Form a green club

Trees constantly give out water into the atmosphere. That is why it is so cool under a tree. Trees also help in increasing rainfall. Plant trees. Tell others not to destroy them.

Make others aware

Water gets polluted through pollutants from sewage and garbage from houses, fields and factories. Convince people that it is wrong to wash and clean near sources of water. The right disposal of wastes gives you clean and safe drinking water.

Purify drinking water

Water can be purified by boiling, filtering and treating with chemicals.

How to make a filter

You will need:
- a plant pot
- some cotton wool
- pebbles
- sand
- charcoal
- a glass
- some muddy water

1. Take the plant pot and plug the hole at the bottom with cotton wool.
2. Put a layer of small clean pebbles at the bottom.
3. Wash some fine sand and make a thick layer above the pebbles.
4. Grind some charcoal into a paste and pour it evenly over the sand.
5. Pour some muddy water onto the layer of charcoal. Collect the clean water in a glass placed below the pot.